the guide to owning a
Python

Jerry G. Walls

T.F.H. Publications
One TFH Plaza
Third and Union Avenues
Neptune City, NJ 07753

Copyright © 2001 by T.F.H. Publications, Inc.

All rights reserved. No part of this publication may be reproduced, stored, or transmitted in any form, or by any means electronic, mechanical or otherwise, without written permission from T.F.H. Publications, except where permitted by law. Requests for permission or further information should be directed to the above address.

This book has been published with the intent to provide accurate and authoritative information in regard to the subject matter within. While every precaution has been taken in preparation of this book, the publisher and author assume no responsibility for errors or omissions. Neither is any liability assumed for damages resulting from the use of the information herein.

ISBN 0-7938-0382-9

If you purchased this book without a cover you should be aware that this book is stolen. It was reported as unsold and destroyed to the publisher and neither the author nor the publisher has received any payment for this "stripped book."

Printed and bound in the United States of America

Printed and Distributed by T.F.H. Publications, Inc.
Neptune City, NJ

Contents

So You Want a Python 5

The Biggest 15

The Best Python Around 28

Diamonds, Carpets, and Greens 38

A Few Other Pythons 52

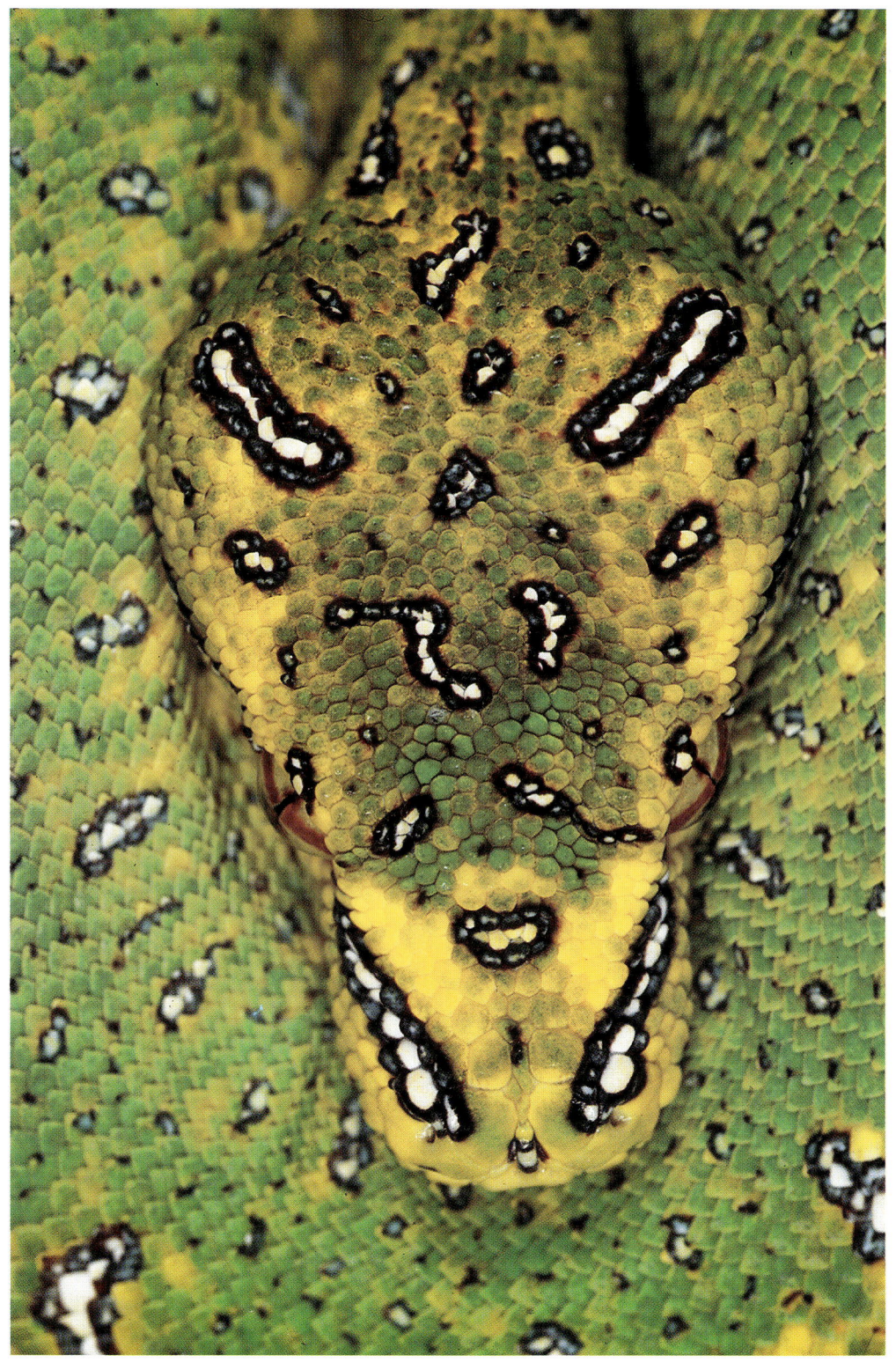

The head pattern of this young male Green Tree Python, *Python viridis*, will largely disappear in a year or less.

So You Want a Python

Today's reptile enthusiasts have available to them a tremendous variety of species of turtles, lizards, and snakes to challenge their husbandry abilities and creativity. Though each of these groups has many admirers, there is little doubt that the snakes are the most popular reptile pets, and of all the snakes the pythons and boas are the most desirable. Yet at the same time, the pythons are incredibly challenging and often dangerous pets that are not suitable for many of the hobbyists who try to keep them.

PYTHONS VERSUS BOAS

Traditionally the "giant snakes"—the boas and pythons—have been treated as a single family, Boidae, with two subfamilies, Boinae for the boas and Pythoninae for the pythons. Unfortunately, this simplistic classification bears little resemblance to reality, and in the opinions of many workers today the Boidae actually is a group of several families that are not provably closely related. For this reason a python to me is a member of a greatly restricted family Pythonidae, one

Reticulated Pythons are readily available but are not good pets for beginners.

Detail of the smooth back scales of a Ball Python, *Python regius*.

consisting of mostly large snakes (seldom under 4 feet [1.2 m] long in adults) with many rows of scales around the back (typically over 25 rows) and ventral scales that are narrow. There is a pair of fused premaxillary bones at the front of the upper jaws that bears teeth (absent in boas) and a hooked bone, the postorbital, at the back of the orbit. The scales of the head vary greatly, from large and regular in placement to tiny and undifferentiated. Both sexes have small remnants of the hind legs present in the musculature near the vent with a claw-like spur projecting through the skin (though sometimes hidden under scales). The eyes have vertical pupils. All species lay eggs; none are livebearers. True pythons are found only in the Old World, in Africa (excluding Madagascar) as well as in southern Asia from India to southeastern China and over the Indonesian islands and New Guinea, then over Australia.

Presently some 28 to 35 species of pythons are recognized as valid by various workers, distributed as follows: Africa: four species; India to Indonesia and New Guinea: 15 species; Australia: 17 species (several occur in both New Guinea and Australia). These species are broken into four major groups (genera) that are thought to share a common ancestor. Arranged by genus, the species of pythons are:

Antaresia: childreni*, maculosa*, perthensis, stimsoni*

Aspidites: melanocephalus, ramsayi

Liasis: albertisi*, barroni, boa*, fuscus*, mackloti*, olivaceus, papuanus, savuensis*

Python: amethistinus*, anchietae, boeleni, bredli, brongersmai*, carinatus, curtus*, imbricatus, molurus*, natalensis, oenpelliensis, regius*, reticulatus*, sebae*, spilotus*, timoriensis, viridis*.

The species marked with an asterisk are relatively easy to find in the hobby and would be available to beginning and moderately experienced hobbyists, though often expensive and not necessarily good pets. Of the 17 species that are fairly easy to find currently, the underlined species generally are considered to make the best pets; they are affordable and are not large enough (typically under 10 feet, 3 meters) to be even potentially dangerous, though they are capable of inflicting painful bites. For beginners, the best pets would certainly be the species of *Antaresia, Liasis savuensis, Python brongersmai, Python regius,* and *Python spilotus*, all of which are bred in captivity in good numbers, have passably calm temperaments, are attractive in coloration and form, and are small enough to be handled by an unaccompanied adult or even a teenager. Detailed information on all the python species, from the largest to the smallest, can be found in my book *The Living Pythons* (T.F.H.), published in 1998.

PROBLEM PETS

You cannot write anything on pythons without being brutally honest—many of the most common and popular, as well as cheapest, pythons are dangerous animals. More hobbyists keep the Burmese Python, *Python molurus bivittatus,* than any other species except perhaps the Ball Python, *Python regius.* These two species coincidentally represent extremes of the family Pythonidae. The Burmese is a true giant among living vertebrates, large females often exceeding 15 feet (4.5 meters) in length and well over 100 pounds (45 kilos) in weight, being capable of reaching 30 feet (9.2 m) and over 300 pounds (136 kilos); few Ball Pythons exceed 5 feet (1.5 m) in length and a few pounds in weight. Obviously Ball Pythons are more suitable or at least less dangerous pets than Burmese Pythons, assuming their behavior is at all similar (as it is), yet young specimens of both species are sold as though the two species were equally keepable. This just is not true, a fact that has to be considered by every hobbyist planning to purchase a python.

It has been suggested (Barker & Barker, 1995, *Vivarium,* 7[3]) that the potential

Many pythons, such as *Python boleni*, are expensive and hard to find in terraria.

danger of a pet python is directly related to its weight. If a python being handled by a typical adult keeper is under some 40 pounds (18 kilos) in weight, with the proper precautions it probably cannot kill its handler. When its weight is more than half the weight of its handler, its extreme muscularity combined with the weight makes it difficult to remove if an accident happens and it can be considered potentially deadly. If a python weighs as much as or more than its handler, there is no doubt that it can kill a single handler. Since a 14-foot (4.2-m) Burmese Python commonly weighs a hundred pounds (45 kilos), any such pet is potentially deadly, and its bite is certainly dangerous. A 14-foot female Burmese Python may be only three years old.

As Burmese Pythons, Reticulated Pythons (averaging somewhat longer than the Burmese but typically more slender at younger ages but more vicious when adult), and African Rock Pythons have become more familiar pets, there have been more incidents of terrible accidents and even deaths resulting from these species. These are not mental giants and they are not vindictive, so accidents result from the carelessness or stupidity of the owner/handler. Classic causes of deaths from python accidents have been due to either allowing a giant python to roam freely around a house (where it can mistakenly consider children as prey) or failing to remove delightful rodent/rabbit smells from the hands or even the throat. Pythons detect prey by scent, react with unbelievable swiftness to bite it, and then if necessary encircle it with coils that constrict more strongly the more the prey struggles. A keeper who foolishly tries to feed a giant python rabbits while either intoxicated or under the sluggishness of drugs is asking for trouble and often gets it; in one case a keeper apparently held a dead rabbit under his chin while opening his python's cage, and the pet failed to distinguish keeper and food—resulting in the demise of the keeper and later the python.

Large pythons are capable of dangerous, bloody bites and cannot be handled without assistance.

BASIC RULES

1) Never bite off more than you can chew when purchasing a python. The species that reach significantly over 10 feet (3 m) in length are not suitable for children, teenagers, invalids, show-offs, or homes with any of the above. This means that

Young albino Burmese Pythons, *Python molurus bivittatus*, are hard to resist, but they quickly grow to a very large size.

Burmese Pythons (*Python molurus bivittatus*), Indian Pythons (*P. m. molurus*), Reticulated Pythons (*P. reticulatus*), African Rock Pythons (*P. sebae* and *P. natalensis*), and Scrub Pythons (*P. amethistinus*) are unsuitable pets for the average household situation.

2) Cage all pythons securely and know where they are at all times. In the case of large specimens, this will mean giving them their own secure room or a room-sized pen.

3) Concomitantly, never allow a large python (or any python, for than matter) to roam a structure where there are or may be other pets, children, uninformed visitors, or uninvited intruders. In fact, it is best to have a secure lock on the door of your python's cage or room and a reinforced, lockable holding area within the room where the python can be confined during cleaning activities.

4) Never try to handle or feed a python over perhaps 10 to 12 feet (3 to 3.6 m) long by yourself. Have an assistant help, preferably with another assistant for every 3 to 4 feet (0.9 to 1.2 m) in length over this dangerous minimum.

5) Be extremely careful when feeding any python—their first reaction to food is to grab it with the long anterior teeth, and some are lousy shots. Their teeth produce bloody bites that can damage nerves and ligaments; if a major blood vessel is ripped when you automatically pull away, you could bleed to death. Once a python grips you, there is no certain way to make it release—every suggested action that may work on other large snakes, such as blowing into the nostrils, holding the head under water, pepper spray, or even trying to cut the backbone, is uncertain. The best bet is to patiently and calmly, with minimal movement, wait for the python to realize

its mistake and release the bite. If you can do this with 40 pounds (18 kilos) of python hanging onto an arm, you are truly cut out to keep large pythons.

6) Protect your eyes while feeding or handling a python. As do several other groups of snakes (spitting cobras among them), there is more than just an incidental selection of the eyes as targets by pythons. This may be because of the rapid blinking of the lids or perhaps because of reflections from the pupil and iris. Either way, never let a python get close to your face; plastic surgery is expensive.

GENERAL CARE SUGGESTIONS

It should be obvious that you cannot cage and handle a 15-foot (4.5 meters) Burmese Python as you would a 3-foot (0.9-meter) Ball Python. At least both these pythons occur in nature in similar habitats, savannas and the edges of forests; other pythons inhabit deserts and perpetually wet rain forests, some live in the trees and others burrow. In most cases, however, their cages will share several features.

Cages

Any cage should be at least 1.5 times the length of the adult python, with a locking lid or door. The smallest species can be kept in large aquariums or fiberglass cages, while the larger species will need securely built cages of glass and wood with a minimum of screening. The lid usually is at least partially screened.

Substrate & Furnishings

Except for desert species that do well on dry sand, provide a loose bedding material that will let the pythons burrow in a bit yet not retain too much moisture while being easy to keep clean. Shredded aspen is good, but so are many other commercial substrates. Larger species commonly are kept on newspaper in simple cages to make cleaning easier—large pythons have large defecations. Almost all species will use a sturdy climbing branch or two, a flat rock for basking, and a water bowl. A snug hidebox (remember that snakes like to have their backs and sides in contact with a firm substance) is necessary for all species though obviously difficult to provide for the giants.

Lights

Basking lights are necessary for almost all pythons, providing the locally higher temperatures necessary for activity. Generally the basking light, an incandescent light in a reflective dome mount or a ceramic heat emitter, is mounted over a flat rock or favorite branch at one corner of the cage while the opposite corner is kept cooler, providing a temperature gradient where the snake can control its body temperature through its position in the cage. In addition, many keepers like to mount one or two full-spectrum fluorescent lights over the cage to give the snake at least a simulation of the UV rays in sunlight. Fortunately, most pythons are not very selective when it comes to the quality of basking lights, with temperature rather than wavelength seeming to be more important. During most of the year the room lights (and often the basking light) are kept on for 10 to 12 hours.

Heat

The warmer corner of the cage usually is kept at 84 to 88F (29 to 31C) during the day and allowed to drop five to ten degrees at night, at least during the summer months. A basking light will raise the temperature to 90 to 95F (32 to 35C) in one corner. Heat usually is provided by controlling the basking light in small cages or by using undertank heating pads (insulated pig blankets in the case of large species) or heating strips. Spot heaters such as "hot rocks" seldom are sufficient for pythons. A thermometer should be mounted at each end of the cage for small species; electronic thermometers with remote probes are especially accurate and now quite affordable.

Humidity

Though a few pythons are semiaquatic and the Green Tree Python (*Python viridis*) requires an unusually moist retreat, most pythons large and small are satisfied with a shallow dish of clean, dechlorinated water from which they will drink and in which they will soak and, unfortunately, defecate. It is important that the cage never become too humid when keeping most pythons, as excess humidity increases the chances of harmful bacterial growth both in the cage (bad smells) and on the body of the snake itself (blisters). Large species tend to be more aquatic than smaller ones (some exceptions) and often soak to help support the weight of their bodies. A specimen that spends too much time soaking may be ill or having trouble shedding. Keep a close eye on how your python spends its days in its cage. A simple humidity gauge mounted in

All the common pythons eat rodents when adult, but some young may demand lizards.

the cage will help keep moisture levels within acceptable limits.

Food

All pythons are carnivores, and almost all feed selectively on warm-blooded prey, largely mammals from rat to rabbit in size. The long front teeth easily penetrate the fur of rodents and the feathers of birds. Only a few species take lizards, frogs, and snakes, and these usually are the prey only of hatchlings. Hatchling pythons typically are fed on mice, rat pups, or rats depending on their size, growing up to accept rabbits and occasionally larger prey such as piglets (in the case of Burmese and Reticulated Pythons). Never give in to the urge to show off the appetite of your pet by feeding it prey that is too large (usually anything much longer than the width of the head is too big and may cause dislocated jaws) or active (even a mouse can eat through the skin and head of a large python, causing severe damage or at least a fear of rodents that may cause the snake to cease feeding). Most pythons can be weaned to accepting frozen, thawed foods. Hatchlings will take one or two rodents per feeding two or three times a week, while large adults may need to be fed only every other week. Commonly keepers feed shortly after defecation, which indicates digestion is finished. Because rats and rabbits are expensive to purchase, they make keeping a larger python difficult for someone on a budget—which must be remembered when considering a python as a pet.

Breeding

Many pythons can be bred in captivity, producing a dozen to two dozen large eggs that are incubated in moist vermiculite at about 86F (30C) for 60 to 80 days. Males as a rule are smaller than females (or at least reach smaller maximum sizes) and have larger, more obvious spurs on either side of the vent. Males have a deeply split penis lying in a pair of pockets behind the vent in the base of the tail; when carefully probed with special metal rods, the probes usually travel at least the length of seven to nine subcaudal scales in males; females have only shallow cloacal gland pockets. Males often fight with each other for breeding rights, which can be dangerous and bloody but does seem to increase the incidence of successful matings. Commonly in November adult specimens in good health and well-fed are separated and placed in smaller quarters

In most pythons (here Blood Pythons, *Python curtus*) the females are significantly larger than the males.

that are somewhat cooler (75 to 81F, 24 to 27C) and darker (lights reduced to eight or nine hours a day) and are given less or no food for about 60 days. After this resting period, which allows the sperm to mature, the snakes are returned to normal keeping conditions and placed together. Mating may occur several times within the first week or two but may not be noticed when it occurs at night. Ovulation occurs about a week after a successful mating (females can store sperm for variable periods) and is marked by a slight, temporary swelling of the posterior part of the body. Gravid females often shed some three weeks after mating, laying their eggs three or four weeks later. Though some of the larger pythons incubate their eggs at temperatures higher than air temperature, using short muscular contractions to produce bodily heat, this seldom is noted in captivity. Eggs almost always are incubated away from the mother to control the temperature and humidity and to prevent having to handle exceptionally aggressive females. Captive-bred pythons adapt well to captivity, rapidly become used to rodent diets, often are less nervous than wild-caught specimens, and may be available in unusual and bright colors and patterns. Always purchase a captive-bred specimen both to make keeping easier and to prevent the drain on natural populations.

THE ORPHAN PYTHON

Because the giant pythons (especially the Burmese and the Reticulated) are so easily

Sexes are best determined by probing, which requires experience and care.

purchased, they often fall into the hands of hobbyists totally unsuited to keeping them. These pythons really should always carry a warning sign telling potential owners of the rapid growth, large adult size, expense of feeding, and danger from bites and constriction of these species. Though common and cheap, they are suitable pets only for advanced hobbyists who can supply them with their special keeping conditions.

By the time one of these pythons is two years old, it may be 9 or 10 feet (2.7 to 3 meters) long and already weigh over 50 pounds (23 kilos). At three years of age it is a mature snake, ready to mate but, in the case of females, still growing significantly. Few beginners expect that a 16- to 24-inch (40- to 60-cm) hatchling will reach such a size so quickly, and it scares them. By the time it is two years old, the snake also is

Female pythons brood their eggs if left alone, but keepers remove the eggs for better humidity and temperature control.

putting a significant crimp in their budget, requiring expensive food in large quantities.

All too often the solution to the problem is to get rid of the snake. A few calls to pet shops and zoos make the owner realize that there is no market for large pythons—pet shops don't sell them and zoos have more than enough for their exhibits. A local herpetological society may serve as an adoption agency for unwanted pets, but how many giant pythons can they realistically be expected to place? The newspapers and TV always give accidents involving pythons prominence, and other family members may become insistent that the dangerous snake has to go. Additionally, many states and cities have laws that specifically classify large pythons as dangerous animals, setting legal length limits that are exceeded before the snake is even two years old. This means that neighbors and the law are breathing down the owner's neck as well. Even homeowner's insurance may be impossible to get. The snake just has to go.

After all reasonable solutions are exhausted, the inevitable happens: the snake is released in a park or forest and left to find its own way, much to the shock of anyone who runs across it later before it freezes to death, starves, or is hit by a car. This of course then leads to even more bad publicity for snake owners in general and often the passage of even stricter laws. The only real solution is for hatchlings of the large pythons to be sold only to owners properly equipped physically, financially, and mentally. Under no conditions should that cute Burmese or Reticulated Python ever be recommended as a beginner's pet.

The Biggest

In this chapter I'm going to talk a bit about five of the longest vertebrate animals ever kept as pets. These are the Asian Rock Python, specifically the subspecies known as the Burmese Python, the Reticulated Python, the African rock pythons (two very similar species), and the Scrub Python. Though the first two are commonly available in the hobby and the last is becoming increasingly so, I personally feel that none of these pythons should be kept by the average hobbyist—they are just too dangerous. So let's get the worst python pets out of the way first and get on to the good stuff.

PYTHON MANIA

It's hard to pinpoint exactly why hobbyists are attracted to pythons over 20 feet long, but I suspect it's a combination of their beauty and the challenge. Burmese Pythons have been familiar pets for years, being well-known as an exhibit in circuses and zoos and even used by snake dancers on a regular basis. However, these snakes are relatively new in the terrarium hobby, with captive-bred Burmese Pythons first becoming common and affordable in the early

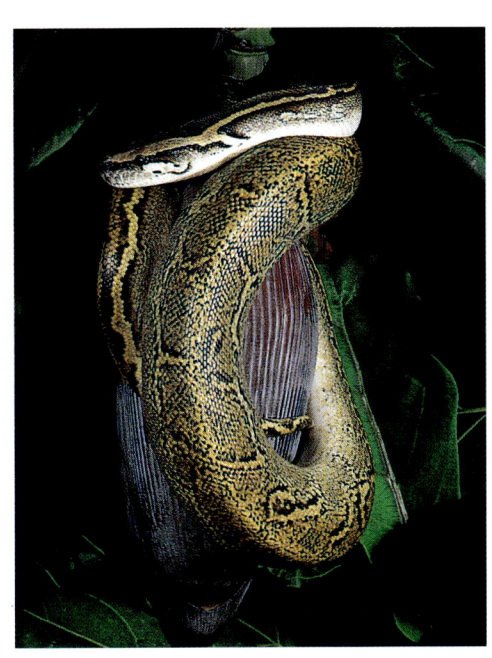

A beautiful variant color pattern of the Burmese Python.

1990s, with albinos being produced cheaply by the middle of the decade. As the price of an albino Burmese dropped, breeder interest in Reticulated Pythons grew and reached a frenzy when the first mutations and captive-bred albinos appeared in the late 1990s. Recently more breeders have been producing Scrub Pythons, but captive-bred African rock pythons remain rare.

All these pythons find a ready market among two levels of hobbyists: advanced keepers/breeders with large facilities and a budget allowing them to profitably breed the giant pythons, and beginning hobbyists who fall under the spell of hatchlings in a pet shop and bite off more than they can chew. If you realize just how large these snakes get and how quickly they grow, and if you have a suitably large and secure caging area and exercise good caution and common sense when handling them, it is not impossible to keep these pythons as pets, but they are under no circumstances to be kept in the average home or where children are present. Make no mistake about it: all five of these pythons are fully capable of killing an adult human by the time they are three or four years old. Keeping even the most "gentle" Burmese Python where children are present is foolish and dangerous, and often against the law.

BURMESE PYTHONS

The snake that most hobbyists call the Burmese Python technically is a subspecies of what is formally known as the Asian Rock Python, *Python molurus*. This species, which is found from Pakistan to southeastern China and south over the western Indonesian islands plus Borneo and Sulawesi (but not the Philippines), generally is held to be composed of two or three subspecies. The western form, *P. molurus molurus*, the Indian Python (Pakistan and India to Assam), has the dark triangle on top of the head fading out at about the level of the eyes, with the front of the head pale; it also has one of the supralabials (upper lip scales) touching the bottom of the eye. On Sri Lanka is found a slightly distinguished form sometimes called *P. m. pimbura* that has the major characters of the Indian Python but a more irregular pattern. Both these snakes are protected and are not legally exported without a great deal of

Small scales under the eye help define the Burmese Python.

THE GUIDE TO OWNING A PYTHON

Python molurus pimbura of Sri Lanka has a more irregular pattern than typical *molurus*.

paperwork, so they seldom are available to hobbyists.

The familiar form of this snake is the eastern Burmese Python, *P. m. bivittatus*, which is found from Burma over the rest of the range of the species. Not only does the brown triangle on top of the head extend forward to the tip of the snout in this subspecies, but there are one or two rows of small scales below the eye that intervene between the lip scales and the lower edge of the eye. This is the only subspecies legally kept and bred by hobbyists today (or at least the only one readily sold across state lines in the U.S.), but some lineages show former interbreeding in captivity with the Indian Python by having a nearly patternless front part of the head. (When it became very difficult to legally sell Indian Pythons, some breeders simply used their Indians as part of their breeding stock of Burmese Pythons rather than waste the animals.)

One of the most attractive snakes, it is pale olive-tan with a series of large, often irregular, squarish dark brown blotches down the middle of the back from behind the nape onto the tail. On the side are smaller brown blotches. The head pattern features a brown triangle formed by the fusion of two wide brown bands that start on the nape. Often there is a pale diamond in the center of the triangle. A wide brown stripe runs diagonally from the nostril through the eye to over the angle of the jaws; it is wider behind the eye than in front (where often very ragged) and behind the eye it is edged below by a large white oval extending onto the jaws; there is a dark brown triangle below the eye. The pattern varies

THE BIGGEST

greatly from individual to individual, and today there are several captive-bred mutations that have become available.

Chief among the captive-bred forms is the albino, which generally is a pale pinkish snake with the brown pattern replaced by pale to bright orange; the eye is bright red. In some albinos the pinkish background color is strongly tinted with lavender. Green Burmese Pythons appear faded brown to olive, with indistinct edges to the brown blotches on the back; some have the blotches reduced to small ovals against a pale olive color, while others are patternless or nearly so, uniformly olive-brown. In granite Burmese the pattern is extremely irregular, broken into hundreds of smaller brown blotches covering the back and sides, often with the head distinctly pale; the background color sometimes is a bright golden tan; albino granites exist. Blond Burmese appear to have less black in the pattern, being a very pale tan (often distinctly yellowish) with an orange-brown blotched pattern. Other mutations and pattern variants exist and are being worked on by breeders.

Average adult Burmese Pythons are gigantic, heavily built snakes with very large heads. Males are distinctly smaller than females, most of their growth stopping when they reach some 9 to 12 feet (2.7 to 3.6 meters) in length at three years of age; females continue growing rapidly for at least another year and commonly are 15 to 20 feet (4.5 to 6 meters) long. The record length for the species seems to be 9.2 meters (30.4 feet), but modern specimens almost never are longer than 25 feet (7.5 meters) because so many of these snakes are collected for

A hatchling green Burmese Python. The dark ovals may eventually disappear.

Albino Burmese Pythons vary widely in tone, from incredibly bright animals to relatively dull ones like this specimen.

the skin and native pharmaceuticals markets in southern Asia. Hatchlings are 20 to 24 inches (50 to 60 cm) long.

As is usual with large snakes, Asian Rock Pythons are sedentary animals that may stay in one protected spot much of their adult lives, preferring areas near game trails and near water where prey, largely mammals but also sometimes birds, can be attacked from hiding. They swim well and often are considered semiaquatic, being seen crossing large lakes and rivers, so most cage setups for this python include a large water bowl or wading pool for soaking.

Albino Burmese Pythons are among the most commonly offered larger snakes, being bred in large numbers and thus available cheaply. They also are very colorful and hard to ignore when hatchlings, but remember that by the age of two they could easily be over 10 feet (3 meters) long and weigh more than 40 pounds (18 kilos), being capable of killing a child. This length also exceeds the "dangerous snake" maximums of many cities and states. Consider carefully before being tempted by a Burmese.

RETICULATED PYTHONS

Often considered to be the longest snake in the world today, with an accepted length of 10 meters (33.3 feet)—a bit more than the longest recorded Asian Rock Python—*Python reticulatus* is a relatively slender species compared to the Burmese Python. However, the largest adults still have gigantic heads and bodies and are fully able to constrict a healthy adult human. This probably is the most dangerous python because of its large size, relative mobility, and extreme (usually) nervousness. Though some breeders rate these as "intelligent" snakes, remember that they have a brain the size of a tablespoon and intelligence is very

THE BIGGEST

Some Reticulated Pythons almost glow in the dark. Notice the dark stripe down the center of the head.

relative. They also are somewhat deceptive in that young specimens may be gentle snakes, but they become progressively more nervous as they mature. The species is found from southeastern China to Burma and then south over Southeast Asia, the Indonesian islands almost to New Guinea, and the Philippines and adjacent islands, including Borneo.

One of the first things you notice about a Retic is the bright orange to yellow eyes, a characteristic of the species along with the narrow black line that runs down the center of the head from between the nostrils to the nape. These two features make almost any Retic recognizable at a glance. Other than a narrow black line from the back edge of the eye over the angle of the jaws, the face is clean, with little or no pattern. The body pattern varies considerably but usually consists of pale brown diamonds running down the center of the back, these formed by dark-edged, pale-centered five-sided rhombs on each side of the body that meet at the center of the back. Commonly the background color is pale tan to brown with dark brown to black markings, the overall coloration brighter anteriorly than posteriorly. The head may be brown to distinctly reddish or yellowish.

Recently a few color mutations of the Reticulated Python have been developed, but none is common yet and they remain expensive. The most affordable may be the striped Retic, in which the dark edges of the rhombs on the sides are fused into continuous or nearly continuous black stripes against a brownish background. In the best specimens there is a black stripe down the center of the back and a pair of stripes low on the sides, but the head pattern remains relatively intact; the centers of the stripes may be distinctly golden. Specimens that are intermediate between the striped and a normal Reticulated are called tiger Retics, having a partially striped pattern with strong traces of the rhombs on the side and sometimes traces of diamonds on the back; tiger Retics currently are quite popular and available. Some breeders believe these snakes remain relatively calm when adult. The other major variety so far produced, though still in very small numbers, is the albino Reticulated Python. At least two types appear to be present, one with a whitish pink background color, the other distinctly lavender. In both the

This juvenile tiger morph Reticulated Python has a nearly complete pattern.

Fully striped Retics still are rare, with most specimens approaching the tiger morph to some extent.

THE BIGGEST 21

dark edges of the rhombs are pinkish blue, the centers usually brilliant gold, with the entire head bright yellow. These beautiful animals currently are excessively expensive. There is repeated talk among breeders of dwarf varieties of Retics being bred, adults not reaching much over 10 feet (3 meters), but such claims have yet to be proved.

Reticulated Pythons are big snakes. Average adults are 10 (males) to 20 (females) feet long (3 to 6 meters) and weigh from 50 to over 200 pounds (22.5 to 90 kilos). These lengths can be reached in as little as two years from hatchlings 28 to 36 inches long.

Sexual maturity is reached at an age of three to five years, the males being distinctly shorter (7 feet, 2.1 meters) and more slender than females (12 feet, 3.6 meters), with longer spurs by the vent and a tendency to fight with other males when mating season approaches. They usually are prepared for breeding by a cooling period lasting from November to February, with only nine or ten hours of

Brilliant orange to golden yellow or even red eyes mark the Retic.

light per day and temperatures at least ten degrees lower than usual. The sexes are reunited for breeding in mid-February. Females may lay over a dozen eggs the size of a grapefruit, these hatching in some 80 days. [For an exceptionally detailed discussion of breeding Reticulated Pythons, see Barker, et al., 1999, *Reptiles*, 7(11).]

Because hatchlings are not much heavier in build than an adult Pine Snake (*Pituophis melanoleucus*) and are seemingly gentle, easily handled snakes, many beginners have purchased baby Retics believing they have a good pet. Few dealers tell unknowing buyers that the snakes will be quadruple or more their hatchling length in a year or two and usually become progressively more nervous and unpredictable. Reticulated Pythons kill or severely injure several careless handlers each year, accidents that could largely be prevented by restricting purchase of these snakes, keeping them out of the hands of beginners.

This 18-foot Retic is eating a 30-pound pig.

Albino Reticulated Pythons remain among the rarest and most expensive of the snakes.

AFRICAN ROCK PYTHONS

At first glance, a typical African Rock Python, *Python sebae*, the rock python found across central Africa from coast to coast, looks much like a slender Burmese Python, with a similar dark brown triangle on top of the head and a brown facial pattern, but with smaller and more regular dark brown blotches on the back. They commonly appear a bit more slender than a typical Burmese of the same size, but some of this may be due to the fact that most specimens seen are imports that have never had the pleasure of regular meals. The top of the head, including the snout, has large, regularly placed scales.

Almost identical at first glance and formerly considered a subspecies of *P. sebae*, the Lesser Rock Python, *Python natalensis*, is the form of southern and southeastern Africa. Its facial, head, and body pattern are weaker and less distinct, especially on the face in front of the eye, and the top of the head is covered with small, irregular scales at least from the level of the eyes back (large and more regular in *P. sebae*). The upper lip scales are pale (not heavily marked as in *P. sebae*) and there is no distinct pale

THE BIGGEST

The most common African Rock Python, *Python sebae*, has fairly large head scales and heavy dark markings in front of the eye.

Lesser Rock Pythons, *Python natalensis*, have little or no dark brown in front of the eye and tiny, irregular head scales. This species rarely is sold.

Beautifully striped African Rock Pythons occur in nature and eventually are certain to be produced through captive breeding.

triangle below the eye as in its relative. Few specimens of this species are seen in captivity at the moment.

Both these species occur in many habitats, from near-desert savanna to forest edges, but usually there is a lake or other large body of water nearby. Like the other large pythons, they may be semiaquatic when the opportunity presents itself, and captives like to soak for long periods in a large pool of clean water. Both species have been noted for their nervousness and their aggressive tendencies, and neither makes a good pet, biting viciously when handled. Adults commonly are 13 to 18 feet (3.9 to 5.4 meters) long, though *P. natalensis* commonly is a third shorter than *P. sebae*.

At least one *Python sebae* has been measured at a bit over 32 feet (9.6 meters) in total length, putting this species in the same league as *P. molurus* and *P. reticulatus*. Both species can be kept much like any other large python.

Hatchlings of *Python sebae* and occasionally *P. natalensis* are imported and may be sold at low prices. These 22- to 26-inch (56- to 66-cm) babies commonly are dark and have very irregular patterns and do not compare in appearance with baby Burmese, but they do find a market. Unfortunately, they start off as biters and remain that way throughout life, making larger adults very dangerous animals. It can be assumed that when captive-bred in larger numbers (which so far is not happening) the African rock pythons will produce striped and albino mutations, both of which already have been reported in rare instances.

SCRUB PYTHONS

Python amethistinus is an unusual, relatively slender, very nervous python whose range includes most of New Guinea (except for the central highlands), adjacent islands, and northeastern Queensland, Australia. In this restricted range it is one of the major predators, large adults commonly exceeding 20 feet (6 meters) in length, with an apparent record of 28 feet (8.6 meters).

In color this is one of the most varied pythons, with three major groups of patterns. They may be uniformly golden brown to reddish brown, dark brown with broken or complete darker crosses over the back, or dark brown with irregular paler and darker brown bands. The head pattern commonly includes dark edges to the scales on top of the head, two or three blackish lines across the back of the head and the nape, and a narrow black band back from the eye to the angle of the jaws. The upper lip scales may be whitish or edged with black. The lines across the back of the head are virtually unique (when present), otherwise being found only in some *Python timoriensis*, a rare species that displays many characters intermediate between Scrub and Reticulated Pythons.

One of the most adaptable of the pythons, Scrubs may live in deserts or rain

Some authorities recognize five species of Scrub Pythons, not all of which have the distinctive black bars across the back of the head.

Rarely available, *Python timoriensis* looks like a cross between a Scrub Python and a Reticulated Python, with features of both species.

forests, with or without trees or large bodies of water. They are excellent climbers and swimmers and not afraid to tackle large prey. When cornered or handled they bite viciously, inflicting deep and painful wounds. Large specimens, though more slender than the other pythons in this chapter, could in theory kill a human if given the opportunity. These are unpleasant captives at best.

Though the Scrub Python is not especially attractive when adult, it does have pretty babies. For several months they may be uniformly bright reddish brown, with just traces of a darker pattern. Like other pythons, however, they grow rapidly and soon attain 9 to 12 feet (2.7 to 3.6 meters) in length and what usually is an irregular dark-on-dark pattern. Adults may be very active, requiring a very large area in captivity; males fight viciously before breeding. There really are few objective reasons to keep this species, but it is bred in captivity on occasion and recently has been assuming a higher profile in the hobby.

The Best Python Around

The question often comes up of which snake is best for a beginner. The standard answer for many years has been the Corn Snake, a colorful, gentle, easily kept species that is bred in captivity in very large numbers and over two dozen colors and patterns. Since the middle of the 1990s, however, a "dark horse" snake has moved into contention as a prime beginner's species: the Ball Python, *Python regius*. Once notorious as a cheap but difficult snake that was a waste of money to purchase, true captive-bred Ball Pythons now are available at reasonable prices to any hobbyist willing to look for a good dealer. Captive-breds have proved to be not only easy to maintain and very long-lived, but they now are produced in nearly as many color varieties as the Corn Snake (though not yet so dramatic or colorful).

Ball Pythons make excellent (and beautiful) pets under certain conditions.

DESCRIPTION

The Ball Python, known as the Royal Python in Europe, is a very common small species found in savannas, gardens, forest edges, and other similar habitats across central Africa from Senegal to Uganda above Lake Victoria. It has maintained large population numbers even near larger native villages, where it sometimes is protected under local religious beliefs. It is a thick-set snake with a rather small

Ball Pythons are individually variable. Most are a bright golden tan and deep brown, with a strong luster. The dark bands vary considerably in width and shape.

Some Ball Pythons are much darker and less lustrous, the golden ovals a dusky tan and the dark markings almost black.

THE BEST PYTHON AROUND

The rare Angolan Python, *Python anchietae*, has distinctly raised scales on top of the head and a more spotted pattern than the Ball Python.

head, short tail, and quite stout body, a very typical python build. The color pattern of the head is distinctive: the entire top of the head is covered by a dark brown triangle that curves down at the back corners to produce a broad dark brown stripe that continues forward through the eye to the tip of the snout. A pale golden band is thus isolated between the top of the head and the eye stripe. The lips are whitish to golden brown, generally unmarked. (This head pattern is shared with the rarely seen *Python anchietae*, the Angolan Python, a very similar species restricted to dry habitat in Angola and Namibia and characterized by a somewhat different body pattern and raised scales on top of the head.) The body of a typical Ball Python is beautifully patterned in golden brown and blackish brown. A dark brown, very irregular stripe runs down the center of the back and sends out about 20 similar bands over each side toward the belly, surrounding broad tan ovals on the side. Typically each oval has one or two small brown spots in it and there may be elongated pale ovals developed in the stripe down the center of the back. Some specimens are brilliantly patterned, almost yellow and black, others much darker, dull brown and black; the pattern itself varies tremendously in details, such as width of bands and pale areas, and it is hard to find two specimens that are identical.

Hatchling Ball Pythons are only some 14 inches (35 cm) long, but they grow as rapidly as do the other pythons, reaching

Commonly there is a continuous narrow middorsal black stripe in Ball Pythons.

sexual maturity in about three to five years. Typical adults are some 42 to 60 inches (1.1 to 1.5 meters) long, females distinctly longer than males. The record length for the species is supposed to be almost 8 feet (2.4 meters), but few specimens even 6 feet (1.8 meters) long are seen today, and captives much over 4 feet (1.2 meters) are exceptional. This size range is much as in many common pet snakes, such as the Corn Snake, and allows the species to be easily handled even by children (under supervision, of course).

BEHAVIOR

Also in the snake's favor is a generally tame, gentle temperament, neither young nor adults biting if handled gently and carefully. When picked up it curls around the hand and forms a tight ball that can be hard to remove and is best just tolerated for a few minutes. Wild specimens may form a tight ball even when just touched, the origin of the common name.

Unlike most pythons, it is a burrower, and this may be part of the reason for its gentleness. Much of its time in nature is spent in shallow burrows with small openings. Grassy areas, gardens, and the edges of second growth forests are preferred, and usually the burrows are inherited from rodents that form their prey. The burrows are used both as daytime retreats (the Ball Python is active mostly after dark, when its prey is active) and as incubators for the eggs. Generally one python lives in a burrow, though it is not uncommon to find a male and female or a female and one or two young together. The burrows are shallow enough that they offer little insulation from the

Occasional specimens of Ball Pythons are broadly striped with gold down the center of the back.

THE BEST PYTHON AROUND

Commercial collectors in Ghana and other western African countries dig adult Ball Pythons from their burrows to offer them for sale.

In some African villages Ball Pythons still are held to be semi-sacred, which prevents random killing and collecting in large numbers.

Large adult female Ball Pythons being held for sale. These specimens may lay eggs initially but seldom feed in the terrarium.

heat, often being 100F (38C) or warmer on the hottest days.

Both males and females wander at night in search of prey, and during the dry season males also look for females. Clutches are small, often only three to five eggs, and are noted for being strongly stuck together soon after laying. Incubation takes the usual eight to ten weeks.

CAPTIVE CARE

Because of their small size, captive-bred Ball Pythons are easy to keep. A baby can be housed comfortably in a 10-gallon (38-L) common glass aquarium with a tight-fitting screen top. Provide it with a couple of inches (5 cm) or more of shredded aspen bedding, a small water bowl, and a hidebox. The pythons will climb, but they don't really need a climbing branch to be comfortable, instead just settling down into the bedding. Fed on frozen, thawed mice and later rat pups, a hatchling will double its length in the first year and can be moved to a 20-gallon (76-L) tank where it could spend the rest of its life in comfort. These are very sedentary snakes that like the tight confines of a burrow or small cage; babies will feed better in tight quarters than in cages that are too large for them.

Like other snakes, Ball Pythons should be given a temperature gradient ranging from about 90F (32C) under a weak basking light kept on for 9 to 12 hours a day to 75F (24C) at the coolest end of the cage. Monitor the temperature carefully

Typical Ball Python clutches consist of only three to five eggs.

and watch the behavior of your snake to see where it is most comfortable in the cage, then rearrange the furnishings if necessary. They do best if kept relatively moist, so mist the cage daily. Unlike most larger pythons, Ball Pythons seldom soak in their water bowls. It is not uncommon for Ball Pythons to live 20 years in captivity, with a record of 49 years in a zoo specimen. (This may be the longest lifetime recorded for a snake.)

CAPTIVE-BRED ONLY

The only catch to keeping a Ball Python successfully is the source of your pet. Currently there still are more snakes imported than are bred in captivity. In western Africa several dealers accumulate gravid females and rob burrows for egg clutches. The females are retained until they lay and then (usually) released. Resulting eggs are hatched in large numbers in the country of origin and then the babies are shipped to American and European markets as "captive-bred" or

An axanthic Ball Python. This morph is common but not very colorful, the golden tones being absent and replaced by gray.

Though they have dropped in price, few albino Ball Pythons are available for the hobbyist. This bright yellow-orange form is the height of the breeder's art.

"farm-raised" young. While these babies may have more of a chance of surviving than do wild-caught adult Ball Pythons (which must *never* be purchased as pets), they often are in poor condition by the time they reach pet shops and may not feed, dying in a few months. They also may have mites and intestinal parasites requiring veterinary attention in an often futile effort to keep them alive.

If you purchase a baby Ball Python that was captive-bred locally, however, you generally are assured of getting a healthy baby of known parentage and free from mites and diseases. It also usually has begun feeding on mice and is ready to keep eating in your cage. The problem is that some dealers still misrepresent imports as truly captive-bred, which they are not. Be patient when looking for a Ball Python and be sure you are getting a real captive-bred. Ask the dealer for photos of the parents and of the hatching clutches. Few breeders can produce many Ball Pythons in a season (because of the very small egg clutches), so the price typically is higher than for imports, something to remember when you see babies being sold at ridiculously low prices.

VARIATIONS

Dealers long ago realized that the Ball Python was phenomenally variable in color and pattern, and strange specimens were avidly accumulated by breeders once the basics of keeping this species were established. The hope was that unusually patterned or exceptionally pretty specimens could be bred to establish profitable lines of Ball Pythons. In some cases this proved possible, in others so far there have been few reproducible results.

Fairly common in the wild are striped Ball Pythons. In these specimens the pale ovals that often occur in the dark middorsal stripe expand into a continuous or nearly continuous pale stripe that often is bright golden tan. Basically the usual dark stripe down the center of the back is replaced by a golden stripe bordered on each side by a narrow dark stripe; the pattern of the sides remains normal. It was hoped that striped would prove to be a breedable pattern, but so far crosses of striped specimens with striped specimens have yielded mostly normally patterned Ball Pythons, so striping could be due to temperature or humidity during incubation.

Also often seen in imported specimens are very dark snakes where the paler background color and the dark stripes and banding are not easily distinguished. In such specimens, which are extremely variable, there usually still are narrow pale tan or gold edgings to all the pattern elements, producing an interesting and sometimes quite attractive appearance.

When the first albino Ball Python was discovered in 1990, a new element was added to the pet future of the species, as albinos are beautiful yellow and white snakes that, if captive-bred, could be sold at high prices. Today albino Ball Pythons are relatively common though still expensive, and they have lived up to their advance press. Most specimens are strongly contrasting golden yellow against a pale pink to nearly white background, with bright pink eyes. (The eyes of normal Ball Pythons are nearly black, darker than in most other pythons.) Several lines of albinos are present in breeding stock, and not all seem to be compatible when bred, so at least for now there still are many questions to answer before you can just put together two albinos and get predictable offspring. What might be called semialbinos also are known, such as the caramel and clown. These snakes may be hatched with fairly normal colors, but as they mature they become paler or almost patternless.

Another problematic variant, and certainly the most unique, is the piebald

Jungle Ball Pythons have accentuated yellow on the sides and narrow black banding.

THE GUIDE TO OWNING A PYTHON

An incredible piebald Ball Python. This pattern is surprisingly constant and now has been bred in captivity but still is very expensive. Notice that this specimen also is striped.

Ball Python. In these specimens, which appear as very rare oddities in nature, the normal color pattern is present on the head and neck, usually near midbody (as one to several large areas of color), and usually on the tail. The rest of the back is screaming alabaster white, absolutely without color or pattern. At first thought to be unreproducible freaks, it now seems that the pattern can be inherited, though little commercial stock is available to hobbyists.

Much more common are axanthic (without yellow) specimens. These animals lack the yellow pigment that helps contrast the different shades of brown in the pattern, producing a snake that is shades of gray and brown. Axanthics are very variable in details and probably represent several genetic lineages, though they can be bred in small numbers. In one type, however, the young are hatched almost black and white and gradually darken by the deposition of brown pigment in pale areas.

Jungle Ball Pythons have greatly accentuated pale areas on the sides, these usually some shade of bright or dull yellow. The dark colors are virtually black. Next to albinos, these may be the most colorful Ball Pythons.

Another dozen varieties of *Python regius* are known at the moment, with a few more produced by breeders or imported as breeding stock each year. Fortunately, however, you don't have to be rich to get a pretty Ball Python, as even perfectly normal specimens are beautiful snakes.

THE BEST PYTHON AROUND

Diamonds, Carpets, and Greens

Sometimes looks can be deceiving. The three pythons covered in this chapter at first glance look quite different, but they actually bear many similarities and probably are closely related because their juveniles look much alike and they have overlapping ranges. Just a few years ago they were assigned to two distinct genera; today all three forms are in the genus *Python* and represent just two species.

Carpet Pythons and Diamond Pythons are placed as very distinctive, interbreeding subspecies of *Python spilotus*, a species ranging from extreme southern New Guinea to extreme southeastern Australia and also sweeping across much of northern Australia. This is a typically Australian species with several close allies in other parts of Australia, but because of Australian laws legal exports are not possible at the current time. Green Tree Pythons, *Python viridis*, are essentially a New Guinea species found over much of this large island and some adjacent smaller islands, also occurring in rain forests of northeastern Queensland, Australia. Though their brilliant green coloration is unique in the pythons, structurally they are not very distinctive from several Australian species and there

Brightly marked black and yellow Jungle Carpet Pythons are truly beautiful snakes.

This young Diamond Python shows considerably more yellow blotching than does an adult and accentuates its resemblance to the Carpet Python.

In most of northern and eastern Australia the Carpet Pythons are olive and sandy tan, not especially attractive. This is the northern subspecies, *Python spilotus variegatus*.

DIAMONDS, CARPETS, AND GREENS

A hatchling Diamond Python with distinctive spotting.

DIAMOND PYTHONS

Let's start at the southernmost part of the range, in the coastal forests of New South Wales, Australia. This is the range of the Diamond Python, *Python spilotus spilotus,* one of the most beautiful pythons and also the most cold-adapted. New South Wales has harsh weather, including ice and snow, during the austral winter (the North American and European summer), and simulating this cold period seems to be the trick to keeping Diamonds healthy and even breeding them in captivity.

Diamonds are slender, very muscular arboreal (tree-dwelling) pythons that average about 5 to 6 feet (1.5 to 1.8 meters) long in males and often reach 7 feet (2.1 meters) in females. They have a remarkable color pattern: on a black to deep green background, every scale of the

seems to be no need to place them in a separate genus. Hobbyists have found that Carpet, Diamond, and Green Tree Pythons all make challenging pets but are highly rewarding when kept correctly.

Typical Diamond Pythons are intensely spotted with yellow on a greenish background and bear little superficial resemblance to typical Carpet Pythons.

40 THE GUIDE TO OWNING A PYTHON

Detail of the head of a Diamond Python. Notice the deep pits in the lip scales typical of this group of pythons.

back and sides has a white to bright yellow spot. These small spots form groups of four to six spots outlined with black, placed in four rows across the back, a larger pair on either side of the midline and a smaller spot low on each side. The groups of spots vary greatly in size and intensity and may be partially fused across the back, but they never form rings around the body as in the closely related Carpet Python found to the north and west. The head is black to dark green with many small white to yellow spots; the lips are white or nearly so, with strong black vertical barring. Though seemingly simple in color, good specimens are truly gorgeous snakes.

If kept at the normal warm temperatures used for other pythons, this snake does poorly in captivity and does not live long. They must be given a long (three months) hibernation period when the temperature is held between 50 and 60F (10 and 16C). According to Stan Chiras [2000, *Reptiles*, 8(4)], a successful breeder of this species, the snakes are last fed at the beginning of November and then dropped to their low temperatures suddenly at the beginning of December. They are allowed no basking lights or

Successfully keeping Diamond Pythons requires cool conditions.

DIAMONDS, CARPETS, AND GREENS

heaters during this period and then are brought back up to normal temperatures (84F, 29C) some 90 days later, when breeding often ensues. Females in nature probably lay only every third year or so, something to be remembered if you try to start a breeding program. The snakes first breed at the usual three to four years of age. Hatchlings are dull reddish brown at first, much like the young of Carpet Pythons.

Because little stock manages to leave Australia and few specimens are bred in captivity, this is one of the more expensive pythons and certainly not for the beginner. It is an active, often nervous and bitey form that needs a large cage (preferably over 6 feet, 1.8 meters, long) that is high enough to allow climbing and a good array of branches. Feed specimens sparsely (Chiras, see above, suggests that overfeeding is deadly for this snake); let it keep its lean looks.

CARPET PYTHONS

Found over much of eastern and northern Australia and barely into southeastern New Guinea, the Carpet Python, *Python spilotus variegatus*, is a marvelously variable python that has gained much popularity since the late 1990s as it has been bred in captivity in large numbers. A slender, muscular, arboreal python that may reach 8 feet (2.4 meters) in length but more commonly is 4 to 5 feet (1.2 to 1.5 meters) long, it usually is reddish brown and yellowish tan in basic colors. The top of the head typically has a pattern of a brown cross, the arms running through the eyes, that is forked at the back of the head and sends a branch down and forward to form a wide brown stripe along the edge of the upper jaw. The body pattern varies greatly, but commonly there are four large pale spots across the back that tend to fuse into larger pale spots that may become complete rings around the back, isolating black-edged reddish brown blotches. Extreme specimens may be bright yellow and black or dull brown and tan.

Because of this variation and the tendency of the snake to form locally uniform populations, some scientists and hobbyists recognize as many as four subspecies of Carpet Pythons. The

A hatchling Carpet Python from Irian Jaya is ringed in shades of brown.

Hobbyist interest in Carpet Pythons centers mostly on the colorful form from Queensland called the Jungle Carpet and recognized as subspecies *cheynei*.

Carpet Pythons often are 5 feet long and can be vicious to handle, but most keepers consider them to be relatively gentle pythons.

DIAMONDS, CARPETS, AND GREENS

A young Coastal Carpet Python, subspecies *mcdowelli*.

Northern Carpet Python, *P. s. variegatus*, would be the form in northern and western Australia, typically a dully colored snake with a more or less ringed pattern. The Coastal Carpet Python, *P. s. mcdowelli*, is an inhabitant of wet forests from southeastern New Guinea to Queensland and south to New South Wales (where it would intergrade with the Diamond Python). *P. s. metcalfei*, the Interior Carpet, is found in forests and dry areas from South Australia to central Queensland. The true gem and most desirable form is the Jungle Carpet Python, *P. s. cheynei*, supposedly restricted to the Atherton Tablelands of central Queensland; this is a relatively small black and yellow python that breeders strive to produce in bright and pure colors. Unfortunately, these supposed subspecies are difficult or impossible to distinguish, and there are records of two or more forms seemingly occurring in the same area. It is likely that there are dozens or perhaps hundreds of locally isolated, slightly distinguishable populations of Carpet Python, each of which has moderately distinctive characters.

When it comes to keeping, Carpet Pythons are fairly ordinary. They like a warm, roomy cage with many climbing

Carpet Pythons may change color several times while maturing, with colors growing duller or brighter in unpredictable ways. This young specimen is rather evenly banded.

The head pattern of the Carpet Python is produced by distinctive bars and spots that fuse to form an open cross with forked arms extending over the face. Expect considerable individual variation.

branches and a water bowl, as well as frequent misting if their ancestors came from wet habitats. As you have seen, one form or another of Carpet Python may be found almost anywhere in eastern and northern Australia, from rain forests to open dry forest, virtually scrubland, so expect you will have to experiment with humidity to make specimens from unknown localities comfortable. Adults feed readily on mice and other rodents as well as chicks, with large specimens sometimes taking young rabbits and rats. Hatchlings may demand lizards for a few months, but fortunately they take common skinks of all types.

Breeding follows a cooling period (not as extreme as in the Diamond Python,

DIAMONDS, CARPETS, AND GREENS

45

given the more tropical range of most Carpet Pythons) as in most pythons. Males may be extremely aggressive, fighting each other over mating privileges. They have very large spurs that usually are toothed above the tip. Females may lay a dozen to over three dozen eggs that hatch in the usual eight to ten weeks, producing 16-inch (40-cm) young. Hatchlings often are dull brownish to reddish with little hint of the colors and pattern of the adult. They develop full pattern slowly and change colors often, something to remember if you really must have that gorgeously colored yearling Carpet—by the time it is adult, it may look very different.

GREEN TREE PYTHONS

The Green Tree Python, *Python viridis*, can be considered the elite of the python family. Of all the species commonly available to hobbyists, it is the most desired, the most distinctive in coloration, and perhaps the most distinctive in keeping requirements. An extremely arboreal python that spends its days hidden among branches, fading into the background, it returns to the ground during the night to hunt. Except for a few populations found in rain forests of northeastern Queensland, Australia, Green Tree Pythons are restricted to New Guinea, where they are found from coast to coast (except for the low, swampy southwestern coastal area), including the central highlands. They have adapted fairly well to the sparse human population of the island and still thrive near small cities, as long as their habitat is not destroyed or they are not over-collected for food and the pet market.

Carpet-like pythons from central and western Australia often are recognized as full species. This is Bredl's Python, *Python bredli*, of the Northern Territory.

This young Northern Carpet Python, *Python spilotus variegatus*, is an albino, so far a very rarely found mutation in this species.

Hobbyists should remember that the eastern portion of New Guinea, the country of Papua New Guinea, is closely allied with Australia and like it legally exports very few animals. The western part of the island politically is allied to Indonesia as the territory of Irian Jaya, which does export legally but under a strict permit system. For many years all legal imports of Green Tree Pythons have come from Irian Jaya, but there are strong suspicions that at least some specimens

DIAMONDS, CARPETS, AND GREENS

A yellow 18-week-old Green Tree Python.

are illegally brought in from Papua and even Australia.

The bright green coloration of *Python viridis* is unique in the family and, as usual for green coloration in snakes, is due to a blue pigment deep in the skin being overlain with a translucent reflective yellow pigment in the superficial skin layers. Together the two produce a visually green color. When blue is missing or reduced, you get a yellow tone; when the yellow is missing or reduced, you get a blue area. There is no true green pigment in this snake, just a layering of two other types of color. There are several reports in the literature of older (especially female) Green Trees seeming to change literally overnight from green to blue over large areas of their body. This could be explained at least in part by loss of or damage to the yellow reflective pigment in the outer layers of skin.

Morphologically *Python viridis* is fairly distinctive in the genus, but not unique enough to be placed in its own genus. For many years it resided in *Chondropython*, considered an obviously close relative of the Carpet Python and related species of Australia but differing in having only a single premaxillary tooth on each side of the upper jaw (sometimes absent), its very prehensile tail, details of head scalation, and the presence of small scales on either side of the groove under the chin that allows the jaws to spread to grasp large prey. Closer examination of these characters has show that they are just differences in degree from the condition in other pythons and not that clear-cut. For that reason *Chondropython* was synonymized with *Morelia*, a generic name applied to Australian pythons with oblique sensory slits on the upper jaw; I consider *Morelia* to be part of Python, and thus the name *Python viridis* results. *Chondropython* is preserved today through the common name "Chondro"

A blue female Green Tree Python. Old females (this one is 17 years old) often turn blue.

When sold, most Green Tree Pythons still are in the yellow (or red) phase. They will retain this color for at least another six months to a year.

applied by many hobbyists to the Green Tree Python.

Green Tree Pythons are relatively short pythons, though heavily built and immensely strong. Most adults are 5 to 6 feet (1.5 to 1.8 meters) long, with a reported maximum length of about 7.3 feet. The head is very large, with a swollen snout caused by a pair of very large scales around the nostrils. These are the only large scales on the head, which otherwise is covered with small, irregular scales from the tip of the snout to the nape and on the face, including the area in front of the eye. In the remarkably similar but not closely related Emerald Tree Boa (*Corallus caninus*) of tropical South America there are enlarged scales on the surface of the snout and on the face, a character easily seen even in very small specimens. An outstanding feature of the Green Tree is its large, brilliant eye. In adults the golden green eye is flecked with black. In juveniles the eye matches the head in color, from reddish to golden yellow, and has a dark band running through its center, continuing the pattern of the dark line on the face that runs from the nostril to the back of the head over the face. With growth this dark line through the eye gradually breaks up into the flecks of the adult eye.

Green Tree Pythons are hatched either bright yellow or bright rusty red (often both in the same clutch), with a series of white spots down the center of the back and smaller white spots on the sides; the white spots often are surrounded by

DIAMONDS, CARPETS, AND GREENS

black, and there may be a brown stripe down the center of the back in some specimens. There is as yet no explanation for the two colors in young, but curiously the same thing happens in the Emerald Tree Boa. Some specimens have a distinct brown head pattern much like that of the Carpet Python. At three to six months of age the bright baby colors begin to change to the adult green, a process that may proceed slowly or rapidly. Specimens from the same clutch, kept under the same conditions, may change colors at different rates, and some specimens retain some yellow throughout their lives. Typical adults are bright green above with bright yellow lips and belly. Many have small white or yellow spots on the sides or down the center of the back, and some have an indistinct pale stripe down the back. Axanthic specimens, lacking yellow and thus wholly blue, are known, but it is not certain if this condition is genetic or a result of feeding or environmental conditions. Some specimens have bright yellow heads (especially old females), and a few retain traces of the brown head pattern of the young, including the stripe from the nostril through the eye. Very few Green Tree Pythons are uniformly unrelieved bright green above.

In nature adult Green Trees feed on native rodents, often coming to the ground at night to hunt. Their very long front teeth presumably ensure that a single strike will grasp prey without losing it while feeding in trees; there is no truth to the long-held belief that the long teeth allow it to grab birds more easily—birds are rare in the stomach contents of wild Green Trees. Young specimens have a black or brown tail tip that is wiggled to simulate a caterpillar and thus attract skinks and other lizards that form the majority of their diet; the shift from a lizard to a rodent diet is rapid, however, and few partially grown Green Trees will refuse rodents.

Keeping Green Tree Pythons can be difficult because of their climbing tendencies, sedentary nature, and thin skin that dries out easily. They are kept in large vertical cages with extensive glass areas but well-ventilated to assure good air movement. Large dowels or horizontal branches are used as perches, these staggered so resting snakes don't defecate on each other. A Green Tree spends the day immobile in a distinctive flat coil, the body hanging below the branch and the head in the center of the coil. They feed best in low light conditions, striking rapidly at food, a hand, or a face—bites from this species may be deep, bloody, and extremely painful, so be careful whenever you are trying to handle this species or put your head into its cage.

High humidity (70 to 80% minimum) is essential to keeping this species, which can lead to some rather complicated and high-tech arrangements. In addition to daily misting, the snakes are provided with several hideboxes placed at various levels in the cage, from floor to near the ceiling. In each hidebox place at least 2 to 4 inches (5 to 10 cm) of moist sphagnum

A typical Green Tree Python. Notice the small scales on the head and the enlarged scales around the nostrils as well as the deep sensory pits. White spots almost always are present.

so the snakes can always have a moist retreat when needed. Several Green Trees commonly are kept together in one cage, one male (very large spurs, shorter and slighter build) to two or three females.

Mating in captivity follows a month or two of cooler, drier conditions (60% humidity, temperature down to 70F, 21C, from the usual 81F, 27C or higher). When the sexes are put together again, mating usually follows, though it may be enhanced by having two males fight in the presence of the female. Male fights may be bloody, however, so they should be staged with great care. Mating usually occurs at night while curled about a perch. The two dozen eggs are laid in a hidebox with sphagnum and hatch in roughly seven weeks after being removed to an incubator where the humidity may be kept at only 60 to 70%. Hatchlings are 11 to 14 inches (28 to 35 cm) long. They reach sexual maturity in two to three years and may live over 20 years (like most pythons).

Though you often see hatchling Green Tree Pythons offered for sale in large numbers at shows and even pet shops, they remain expensive snakes and their care may be too complicated for the average hobbyist. Only captive-bred specimens should be purchased—avoid wild-caught imports, which probably are used to feeding on specific rodents you cannot supply and may be carrying large numbers of intestinal parasites. A breeder will be able to help you correctly set up a terrarium for your purchase and can guide you through any problems that may come up, such as maintaining proper humidity. Try to always remember that they have a very quick, bad bite. Keeping a Green Tree is a true challenge, which may be one of the reasons these beautiful snakes have such a large following in the hobby.

DIAMONDS, CARPETS, AND GREENS

A Few Other Pythons

Though there are 30-plus species of true pythons in the family Pythonidae, the several species we've covered so far represent perhaps more than 75% of the species likely to be seen in pet shops and at smaller shows, and all belong to the genus *Python*. One other *Python* species is growing in popularity so it is seen in shops on occasion as captive-breds, while representatives of the genera *Antaresia*, the pygmy pythons, and *Liasis*, the thin-skinned pythons, have a potential place in the terrariums of beginning and intermediate keepers. The fourth genus of pythons, *Aspidites*, is a highly specialized group of academic interest to most keepers as they are among the most expensive of all the pythons. We'll briefly go through this mix of species just to let you know that they exist and also to point out that some might not make bad pets.

BLOODY SHORT-TAILS

Python curtus has been called both the Blood Python and the Short-tailed Python, the first name referring to the dried blood coloration of one form of the

Blood Pythons often are brilliant golden tan; this is subspecies *brongersmai*.

On Borneo the Blood Pythons are duller in color, often just shades of brown. They represent the subspecies *breitensteini*, a member of the Short-tailed Python group.

Dark, nearly black heads may occur in any *Python curtus*, not just in *brongersmai*. Dark heads may come and go with breeding condition and seasons.

A FEW OTHER PYTHONS

species and the latter name in reference to the extremely short tail of adults. This exceedingly heavy-bodied python reaches a length of only 4 to 5 feet (1.2 to 1.5 meters) in typical adults (with a maximum length supposedly of an almost unbelievable 9.9 feet, 3 meters), with the small, cleanly patterned head tiny in comparison to the diameter of the body. The pattern is variable but usually consists of a brown to red background color marked with large golden ovals down the center of the back and on each side, the latter with black centers. The top of the head is coppery brown (sometimes bright gray) with a dark brown face and broad band behind the eye onto the side of the neck. A narrow pale stripe angles down from the eye to the corner of the jaws, breaking the dark coloration of the face into two areas. There is a narrow dark line down the center of the crown, usually trapping a pale oval at the back of the head and with short arms behind the level of the eyes. The entire coloration and pattern is neat and clean, often very sharply defined.

A species of wet, usually muddy areas near lakes, rice fields, and swamps, *Python curtus* occurs from southern Southeast Asia over the Malayan Peninsula and on Sumatra and Borneo. In this area two well-defined forms, now often considered full species rather than subspecies, occur with distinct ranges. The true *Python curtus*, which is grayish brown to golden tan (shades of brown) and has a single large scale over the eye, occurs on Sumatra and Borneo, being absent from the highlands of the islands. *Python brongersmai*

Young *Python curtus* are incredibly stout snakes with very short tails. This body type, so distinctive among the pythons, is retained into adulthood.

Blood Pythons have a bad reputation among keepers for a vicious temper and painful bites. Captive-bred specimens may be more gentle, but caution is advised in handling.

(traditionally considered a subspecies of *P. curtus*) is confined to the mainland, from the tip of the Malayan Peninsula north into southern Cambodia and Laos. It usually has a bright reddish brown color not unlike that of dried blood and has two large scales over the eye. Recent studies have show that the two forms are distinct morphologically and genetically and have non-overlapping geographical ranges, so they readily qualify as species under modern definitions. Both forms are in the hobby, and both are captive-bred in small but growing numbers. *Python brongersmai*, to which the name Blood Python is best applied, is more attractive than the duller brown *Python curtus*, the Short-tailed Python.

Both species are easy to maintain in the terrarium when kept very humid, with a large bathing bowl, and warm, over 86F (30C). These are very inactive snakes that do not need a large terrarium, but they should have a deep, soft substrate in which to rest. Adults feed on the usual variety of rodents, but hatchlings may not eat for over a month after hatching and often go on hunger strikes. Breeding in captivity is not common, but it often follows a dry resting period and then a simulation of a heavy rainy season.

Because *Python curtus* is not a giant species, you might expect it to make a fairly good pet. However, it is heavy for its length and not that easy to handle, being a very strong constrictor. It also has the reputation of being one of the most nervous and unpredictable pythons, striking at the least disturbance and often aiming for the face. Its bite is very painful and bloody, and hatchlings are just as nervous as adults. Though some breeders

A FEW OTHER PYTHONS

Macklot's Python is one of the dullest of the pythons, but it does appear in the terrarium.

say that individual specimens of *Python curtus* and *P. brongersmai* are gentle as lambs and easy to handle, this is not the average experience with these snakes. As captive-bred specimens become more available at lower prices (wild-caught specimens often are heavily parasitized and must be vetted), they will become more tempting to beginners as a pet python because of their small size, but their unpredictable temperament must always be kept in mind.

THIN-SKINNED PYTHONS

The genus *Liasis* contains at least eight species of small to moderately large pythons found from Indonesia over New Guinea and into Australia. Several species are imported for the hobby and a few are bred in captivity with some regularity, though none is especially common or inexpensive. As a rule these are relatively slender pythons with small heads and nearly uniform body coloration in shades of brown. Most, such as the sometimes captive-bred *L. fuscus*, the Australian Water Python, are semiaquatic or at least are often found near water, so the genus

This young adult Australian Water Python, *Liasis fuscus*, is more colorful than most. This brown species often has a rainbow-like iridescence.

THE GUIDE TO OWNING A PYTHON

often is tagged as the "water pythons." The dull coloration of most species makes them unappealing to beginning hobbyists, but two species are attractive (at least when young) and relatively small, and these are captive-bred in fair numbers.

Liasis savuensis, the White-eyed Water Python, is a small species, adults seldom exceeding 2.7 feet (0.8 meter) in length, with an apparent record length of about 6.6 feet (2 meters). Closely related to Macklot's Python, *Liasis mackloti*, from Timor and vicinity (a larger species that is heavily blotched with white and tan in adults and has a dark eye), it is restricted to the island of Savu (Sawu) west of Timor and is easily recognized by the striking white eye in adults (pale golden orange in hatchlings). Young specimens are bright brick red with a grayish head, but as they grow they become brown with darker and lighter specks. This python is not a strong climber and is easily housed in a small terrarium kept at 86 to 90F (30 to 32C) at the warm end. They feed on mice and other rodents and adapt well to captivity. Hatchlings are only 12 to 14 inches (30 to 35 cm) long, but since captive-breds still are uncommon, wild-caught adults are more likely to be seen. This species has a reputation for being gentle and easy to handle, but remember that it is a python and can still pack a bad bite if annoyed.

Hatchling White-eyed Water Pythons are bright red to reddish brown with little or no dark spotting.

An adult *Liasis savuensis* displays contrasting white eyes on a dark head.

Probably the most colorful python is the Ringed Python, *Liasis boa*, sometimes called the Halloween Python. Hatchlings and young specimens often are seen for sale, their brilliant clean orange and black patterns never failing to draw attention. The glossy black head is followed by a wide bright orange band and then alternating black and orange rings, all accented with a high gloss. Some captive-bred lines have the black greatly reduced, forming just black ovals on the sides and leaving the back entirely or nearly all orange. As these pythons grow, however,

A FEW OTHER PYTHONS

White-eyed Water Pythons are slender and typically less than a yard in length. Most are relatively tame, but even these small pythons can give a bad bite.

more and more dark pigment develops in the orange areas, until most adults (5 feet, 1.5 meters) are a motley dark and light brown with a darker head, some touches of orange, and a high gloss. Few dealers display adult specimens when trying to sell this species, because they would prefer that buyers think the brilliant juvenile colors last forever rather than dirtying out at six months to a year in age.

Ringed Pythons are confined to the Bismarck Archipelago off northeastern New Guinea, where they can be fairly common. This is a terrestrial species that lives in moist forests and feeds at night on rodents and perhaps birds. They are easy to keep in a small terrarium with a water bowl and a hidebox, but give them a distinct drop in temperature at night from the normal 86 to 90F (30 to 32C) maintained at the warm end of the terrarium. Young specimens are gentle and even when they bite cause little damage, and most adults are relatively gentle and easy to handle. Unfortunately this species still is moderately expensive

The White-lipped Python comes in two basic forms: with a golden brown back and contrasting black head, and specimens uniformly blackish brown above. The lips are always sharply marked.

A couple of juvenile Ringed Pythons. Individual variation in pattern is enormous, but almost all adults turn dark.

The strong contrast of black head and bands to bright day-glow orange background has led many keepers to call *Liasis boa* the Halloween Python.

A FEW OTHER PYTHONS

when captive-bred (the only way to buy them is as 12-inch, 30-cm, young), as they add nice variety to the captive pythons. Remember, however, that the incredibly colored young you see will soon turn into a rather dull adult.

Closely related to the Ringed Python, though you wouldn't think so at first glance, is the White-lipped Python, *Liasis albertisi*, which is found over most of New Guinea except the central highlands. This extremely glossy blackish brown to honey-brown python has bright white lips densely barred with black, a very attractive pattern. Adults are 6.6 to nearly 10 feet (2 to 3 meters) long. Unfortunately it is seldom bred in captivity, is relatively delicate, requiring consistently high humidity, and has a reputation as a nervous snake that bites with little provocation.

PYGMY PYTHONS

Australia is home to about half the species of pythons known, with all four genera occurring on the continent. Two of the genera of pythons are found only on Australia, both very specialized and atypical. The pygmy pythons, four species of *Antaresia*, are unique little animals that are easy to keep but not easy to breed and are not much larger than a typical Corn Snake, and not much heavier in body build either. Few specimens reach 3.3 feet (1 meter) in length, and they have a small head that is not very distinct from the neck. The sensory pits that are so strongly developed in the lip scales of more typical pythons are weakly developed in these snakes, which are burrowers and hiders in a variety of habitats from dry desert through open woodland to moist forest. All are some shade of brown with

Rough-spotted Pythons are among the smallest species of the family, not much longer or stouter than a yearling Corn Snake, and are gentle and easy to handle.

darker spotting or blotching on the back and little or no head pattern. Their dull colors probably are the main reason they are not more popular as pets, as they are easy to keep in a small terrarium at normally warm temperatures and moderate humidity, and they usually feed on rodents, though hatchlings may prefer lizards for a while.

Two species are fairly easy to find, always as captive-bred specimens (remember that Australia does not allow legal exportation), and they are not easy to distinguish. Fortunately, they can be kept under identical conditions, and they probably have been hybridized by breeders in captivity. The most common probably is *Antaresia maculosa*, the Rough-spotted Python of eastern Australia, which has many very irregular-edged dark brown spots in several rows over the back. Most adults are 24 to 28 inches (60 to 70 cm) long. The Faded or Children's Python, *A. childreni*, is found in much of northern Australia and has more even-edged brown spots on the back, usually barely contrasting with the background color and in even rows. It also is some 24 to 28 inches (60 to 70 cm) long in adults, which may have a distinctly purplish tone. Less common is the desert-dwelling *A. stimsoni*, the Blotched Python, which occurs over the vast expanse of central and western Australia. In this species the brown blotches are large and well-defined, often much darker than the pale brown background color.

Children's (Faded) Python has a simple pattern that often is hard to discern.

The pygmy pythons deserve much more attention from hobbyists than they now get. Though their colors are not bright, they are gentle snakes and easy for any hobbyist to maintain. Though hatchlings, because of their small size (12 inches, 30 cm, or smaller and quite thin-bodied), may be difficult to start feeding and could require skinks and other lizards as a first food, adults are easy snakes. Even if they should bite they seldom do more harm than a Corn Snake bite, and most adults are not especially nervous. Captive-bred hatchlings are relatively inexpensive when you can find them.

ASPIDITES: THE DESIRABLE ODDBALLS

Australia is home to the two species of *Aspidites*, large, slender pythons adapted for burrowing. In the course of learning to live underground they have lost the sensory pits in the lips and have lost the premaxillary teeth (at the tip of the upper jaw) found in all other pythons. Their heads are slender, with relatively small,

A FEW OTHER PYTHONS

A young Black-headed Python. This expensive python retains much the same pattern into adulthood.

dark eyes, and the color pattern consists of narrow dark brown or blackish rings around the back and sometimes onto the belly against a very pale tan to golden tan background. In the Black-headed Python, *Aspidites melanocephalus*, of northern Australia the head and neck are glossy black, while in the Ramsay's Python or Woma, *A. ramsayi*, of central Australia the head and neck are golden brown to distinctly orange. Both species are distinctly ridge-backed like a cobra rather than cylindrical or flattened as in other pythons. Both species are 5 to 6.6 feet (1.5 to 2 meters) long, occasionally reaching almost 10 feet in length (3 meters).

At the moment these are perhaps the most expensive pythons available to hobbyists, and few are seen even at large shows. Australia does not allow legal exportation, and the legality of most hobby specimens could be questioned. Few captive-breds are produced. These are active, nervous pythons that, though not exceptionally bitey, are big enough to cause serious bites. Black-headed Pythons in nature feed mostly on other reptiles, both snakes and lizards, but both species take rodents in captivity. If the price should ever drop so these snakes become affordable for an average keeper, detailed care information should by then be available from their breeders. At the moment, the usual rule is to keep these pythons in moderately large terrariums that are relatively dry and warm, usually offering them a sand or newspaper substrate that parallels their sparse, dry natural habitat.

As we have seen, the pythons are a very variable group with both dangerous giants and gentle pygmies, desert-dwellers and species requiring rainforest humidity. They range from bright green and orange to the dullest monotone browns, and from nervous to relatively non-aggressive. There is something here to please almost any keeper, from beginner to expert, and captive-bred specimens of at least half a dozen species are easy to find. If you display some common sense in making your selection, avoiding the dangerous species, a python can make an excellent pet, even for a beginner.

Index

Bold page numbers indicate photographs

African Rock Python 23-26, **24**, **25**
Albino Ball Python **35**, 36
Albino Burmese Python **8**, 18, 19, **19**
Albino Reticulated Python **3**, 20, 22, **23**
Angolan Python 30, **30**
Antaresia 60-61
Antaresia childreni 61, **61**
Antaresia maculosa **60**, 61
Asian Rock Python .16-19
Aspidites 61-62
Aspidites melanocephalus 62, **62**
Aspidites ramsayi 62
Australian Water Python 56, **56**
Axanthic Ball Python **34**, 37
Ball Python, ...**6**, 28-37, **28**, **29**, **31**, **32**, **33**
Ball Python, Albino **35**, 36
Ball Python, Axanthic **34**, 37
Ball Python, Jungle **36**, 37
Ball Python, Piebald 36-37, **37**
Ball Python, Striped **31**, 36
Black-headed Python 62, **62**
Blood Python **1**, **12**, 52-56, **52-55**
Boidae 5
Bredl's Python **46**
Breeding 12-13
Burmese Python **8**, **14**, **15**, 16-19
Burmese Python, Albino **8**, 18, 19, **19**
Burmese Python, Green **16**, 18, **18**
Cages 10
Carpet Python 38-46, **38-45**, 47
Carpet Python, Coastal **42**, 44, **44**
Carpet Python, Interior 44
Carpet Python, Jungle **38**, **43**, 44, **44**, 45
Carpet Python, Northern **39**, 44, 47
Children's Python .61, **61**
Chondro 48
Chondropython 48
Coastal Carpet Python **42**, 44, **44**
Cycling 12-13
Dangers 7-10
Diamond Python **39**, 40-42, **40**, **41**
Disposing of pet pythons 13-14
Faded Python 61, **61**
Food 12
Genera of pythons 6
General care 10-13
Green Burmese Python **16**, 18, **18**
Green Tree Python **4**, 46-51, **48**, **49**, **51**

Halloween Python 57-60, **59**
Handling 7-10
Heat 11
Humidity 11-12
Indian Python 16
Interior Carpet Python 44
Jungle Ball Python **36**, 37
Jungle Carpet Python **38**, **43**, 44, **44**, 45
Lesser Rock Python 23-26, **24**
Liasis 56-60
Liasis albertisi **58**, 60
Liasis boa 57-60, **59**
Liasis fuscus 56, **56**
Liasis mackloti **56**, 57
Liasis savuensis 57, **57**, 58
Lights 10-11
Macklot's Python **56**, 57
Northern Carpet Python **39**, 44, 47
Piebald Ball Python 36-37, **37**
Problems 7-10
Pygmy pythons 60-61
Python amethistinus 26-27, **26**
Python anchietae .30, **30**
Python boleni 7
Python bredli **46**
Python curtus **1**, **12**, 52-56, **52-55**
Python curtus breitensteini 53
Python (curtus) brongersmai **1**, **12**, 52-56, **52**, **53**, **55**
Python molurus **8**, 16-19
Python molurus bivittatus **8**, **14**, **15**, 16-19, **16**, **18**, **19**
Python molurus molurus 16
Python molurus pimbura 16-17, **17**
Python natalensis 23-26, **24**
Python regius **6**, 28-37, **28**, **29**, **31**, **32**, **33**
Python reticulatus **3**, **5**, **11**, 19-22, **20**, **21**, **22**, **23**
Python sebae 23-26, **24**, **25**
Python spilotus 38-46, **38-45**, 47
Python spilotus cheynei **38**, **43**, 44, **44**, 45
Python spilotus mcdowelli **42**, 44, **44**
Python spilotus metcalfei 44
Python spilotus spilotus **39**, 40-42, **40**, **41**
Python spilotus variegatus **39**, 42-46, 47
Python timoriensis 26, 27
Python viridis **4**, 46-51, **48**, **49**, **51**
Pythonidae 5-6
Ramsay's Python 62

Index

Retic, see Reticulated Python
Reticulated Python (Retic) 3, 5, 11, 19-22, 20, 21, 22
Reticulated Python, Albino 3, 20, 22, 23
Reticulated Python, Striped 20, 21
Reticulated Python, Tiger 20, 21
Ringed Python 57-60, 59
Rough-spotted Python 60, 61
Royal Python 6, 28-37, 28, 29, 31, 32, 33
Safety rules 8-10
Savu Python 57, 57, 58
Scrub Python 26-27, 26
Short-tailed Python 1, 12, 52-56, 52-55
Species of pythons 6
Sri Lankan Python 16-17, 17
Striped Ball Python 31, 36
Striped Reticulated Python 20, 21
Substrates 10
Thin-skinned pythons 56-60
Tiger Reticulated Python 20, 21
Water pythons 56-60
White-eyed Water Python 57, 57, 58
White-lipped Python 58, 60
Woma Python 62

Photo Credits

Marian Bacon: 15; 49

Joan Balzarini: 31 top

R. D. Bartlett: 17; 18; 21 bottom; 22 top; 24 bottom; 25; 34 bottom; 39 bottom; 43 bottom; 45 top & bottom; 52; 60

Allan Both: 56 top; 61

Walter J. Brown: 28

Marius Burger: 24 top

David Dube: 16; 31 bottom

Isabelle Francais: 11; 12; 13; 34 top; 41 bottom; 55

Paul Freed: 21 top; 40 top; 42

James E. Gerholdt: 3 (Python reticulatus, albino); 19; 22 bottom; 23; 29 bottom

Steve Gorzula: 32 top & bottom; 33

Barry Mansell: 27

Gerold & Cindy Merker: 1 (Python curtus brongersmai); 41 top; 53 bottom; 58 bottom

J. Mitchell: 8

John C. Murphy: 5

Aaron Norman: 29 top

Tim Rice, court. Professional Breeders: 35

Mark Smith: 7; 37; 40 bottom

Robert G. Sprackland: 57 bottom

Karl H. Switak: 4; 6; 14; 26; 30; 38; 39 top; 43 top; 44 top; 46; 47; 48 top & bottom; 51; 53 top; 54; 56 bottom; 58 top; 59 top & bottom; 62

John Tyson: 9; 44 bottom

Maleta Walls: 20; 36; 57 top